MW00978891

THE SONG COLLIDES

BOOKS BY CALVIN WHARTON

Poetry
Visualized Chemistry (chapbook)

Short Stories
Three Songs by Hank Williams

Non-fiction
Rowing (with Silken Laumann)

Anthology
East of Main
(co-edited with Tom Wayman)

THE SONG COLLIDES

[poems]

Calvin Wharton

Anvil Press | Vancouver | 2011

Copyright © 2011 by Calvin Wharton

Anvil Press Publishers Inc.
P.O. Box 3008, Main Post Office
Vancouver, B.C. V6B 3X5 Canada
www.anvilpress.com

All rights reserved. No part of this book may be reproduced by any means
without the prior written permission of the publisher, with the exception of
brief passages in reviews. Any request for photocopying or other reprographic
copying of any part of this book must be directed in writing to ACCESS: The
Canadian Copyright Licensing Agency, One Yonge Street, Suite 800, Toronto,
Ontario, Canada, M5E 1E5.

Library and Archives Canada Cataloguing in Publication

Wharton, Calvin, 1952-
          The song collides / Calvin Wharton.

Poems.
ISBN 978-1-897535-68-4

          I. Title.

PS8595.H27S65 2011   C811'.54   C2011-901550-1

Printed and bound in Canada
Cover design by Derek von Essen
Interior design by HeimatHouse

Represented in Canada by the Literary Press Group
Distributed by the University of Toronto Press

  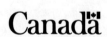

The publisher gratefully acknowledges the financial assistance of the Canada
Council for the Arts, the Canada Book Fund, and the Province of British
Columbia through the B.C. Arts Council and the Book Publishing Tax Credit.

*For Lian and Sean
and in memory of Doreen Wharton*

All of them believed that, having teeth,
feet, hands and language,
life was only a matter of honor.

—from "Those Lives" by Pablo Neruda
Trans. by Alistair Reid

CONTENTS

THE GATE

BORROWING SCENERY

EXIT

THE GATE

AMOUR VERT

Sun swings once more to equinox, the green
of Coltrane's sweet tenor sax,
a breeze written in B-flat.
This is the bursting time: a push upwards
takes the place of old footstep rested now,
heroics of another era
slip further into memory.

The supreme note hears itself and knows how right it is.

A swell of sea water up from fields below the rock.
Birds lever out into open sky, dreaming of the possible—the lush life
of heights. Here, the taste of plum blossoms everywhere,
as if this old standard were something new. The reed vibrates. Brass
and a rush of air asks:

Must this melody end with a question?

FRIEND

He fling monkey talk. Banana talk. Brother walk, though no relation. He spend jazz time, 6/8 time on honey/funk six strings. Vintage, maybe. Years grow tall, like trees. Branches and leaves, then branches and leaves.

Imagine a specific rhythmic pattern to the days, then take it apart, like peeling an orange and separating the sections, sweet on the back of the tongue where memory connects: a long bright chord with vibrato.

Mumbo jumbo mojo in a #sus4. It have plenty more where that come from. He living far away and still I hear his voice, and it make me laugh. Real laugh. All that monkey talk, brother.

JOY

In the breaks between breath
I slide under Beethoven's rolling pin of music,
get baked into a pie with all those songbirds
singing "Freude, Freude"
and clear joy that disturbs
the placid surface of the familiar.

A spring afternoon with my son
is my balance, and we take the bikes,
wheels on concrete to park, to school
and back. The ripple in the treble clef
opens new scenarios for this formation salad
in which we are lettuce or tomato or
something less common, perhaps,
but maybe not better in taste.

The tip of my tongue rings with coppery bitterness,
which gradually dissolves.
Sun settles into a new routine,
as if its cadence might be measured,
as if it had a subtext. Tonight
I will dream of houses and trees
and the mouth of Deep Cove,
a place where possibility dwells
if only for a dreamy moment.
Boy sings a nonsense lyric, plays the melody
one-handed on the piano, and somehow
this becomes the anthem for the day.
A song of you know what.

BLACK AND WHITE

as if the bright day, sunlight sharp on water, trees,
everything in sight
could be the result of collective wishes,
a perfume of thought that changes weather

or the position of the viewer's eye
creates the one who is watched,
this instinct is the true chemistry of the photograph,
and extends picture beyond frame

into the arm of the person holding the print,
self-consciously fills the space from head
to toe, the precise moment of imagining
what shapes the camera reveals

something taken, or given,
while back-lit clouds move slowly overhead.

BEND

Spiral coil creature
on the beach among pebbles
splintered seashell remains,
a term for the physically insignificant;

beneath rain and pungent brine,
a branch of the family tree,

a twist in the program, de-ranged current,
when considered altogether might be

the first and final word

● ● ●

spring salmon swim all year
through tidal rivers
carrying messages, bound instruction,

what is remembered and forgotten,
grains of sand, gelatin crystals,
a god's eye in each and a rope ladder
descending and rising into the mist.

MURDER IN THE HEART

On this otherwise brilliant morning, the SkyTrain
experienced fifteen unscheduled minutes of commuter tranquility,
"a medical emergency at Main Street station"
was all the speaker spoke,
while light shone through an actual-size photo
of some basketball hero's hand,
illuminating a security guard's blue nylon jacket.

Passengers claiming more complete knowledge
insisted suicide, an unknown
jumper had crossed the yellow line
into the face of morning rush hour,
sixty kilometres per hour and the weight of public transit.

I wish I could report that everywhere around me, people
took out notebooks and pens to reconstruct
countless pure renditions of this moment,
but no one had the heart for commentary
unless you count the man with a nose
like the prow of a ship,
his complaint: that whoever it was
could have chosen a more convenient
means to an end,

as if at that moment,
of everything stopping briefly, then beginning again,
the sun could rise once in the west
while we arrive, depart, forget.

TOOTH FAIRY

My son, giddy with a six-year-old's delight
at toothlessness, four teeth out in ten days

the front of his mouth empty in the mirror,
a doubling of his surprised laughter,

finally asks questions about the tooth fairy,
where she gets her money, how

she enters people's houses; I tell him
it's like Santa Claus (intending magic)

but he says: *you mean she comes down the chimney?*
and because I don't want him to lose these mysteries yet

I concoct a tale of getting in through open windows,
bearing coins in exchange for unwanted incisors

leaving messages under his pillow, her hand
as it lifts his beautiful child head

so gentle it never wakes him from his dream.

JOKE

Have you heard the one about the travelling St. Peter
who put velcro tape on a rooster's ass then jumped
from the top of the Empire State building into a herd
of elephants wearing suspenders until Tarzan took off his
sunglasses the better to see a chicken dart into the roadway
and in the meantime the farmer's sons have been digging a hole
in a field discussing hamsters wrapped in electrician's tape
and every few minutes one of them steps outside the circle
to screw in a light bulb so the sunburned penguin turns to
the American and says, "You know, Superman, sometimes
you can be a real prick."

THE FUNNEL

Collection of what stands alone,
mirror magnification:
     caught or carried
       between us   moment or motion

light's return from surface
revelation of scene
as "seen"

    tricks on us,
no unblemished point of view

as purposely spastic eyes
in Japanese art.

            ◉   ◉   ◉

World enters, whole,
the funnel
re-creates
synthetic consistency, logic construct

what we use
to measure each against other,
for example
the way we all speak
a foreign language.

            ◉   ◉   ◉

Ripe apples and pears hang
hold elastic wooden branches
                green leaves turning
the weight of autumn
simply of earth grown,
and reaching now
from sky to ground,
the offer:
eat and the whole world
down your chin
out your smile
in your eyes not
through them.

WHEN "X" NO LONGER EQUALS "Y"

Deft stroke of voice from across the continent,
the only brother says he knows the worth of himself,
recognition of habitual falling (or standing) down
a waist-high pile of cheeseburgers, onion rings
and always put aside today for eventually what?

She goes out the door, choosing the sociopath,
thinks she can still send orders maybe in the mail,
cigarette ash accumulates on a glass plate

while possibly the daughter, the child who may utter
but cannot articulate for herself,
takes the most grievous hurt
which he, father (brother), at least considers—
good life constructs itself from solid materials.

●   ●   ●

He levels the voice with which he speaks,
perks up days later to become more angry;
a full moon imbalances a thick fulcrum line of cloud,
but back at his house the woman has departed
furniture and child replaced by a foolscap sheet of claims,
the first night of summer cancelled by uncertainty.

Panic and bad counsel terrify her thoughts,
the mother (wife) pinpoints a system of complaint,
not compliant, finds the source of failure outside herself.

The child has no convention to follow,
a series of future events which will reveal themselves,
she (daughter) lacks the investigative vocabulary,
lives in a three-year-old universe suddenly without standards,
an active becoming grows the appendage of doubt
as if it were a type of reward or punishment.

◉   ◉   ◉

The conjunction of two lines occurs only once
unless they are parallel and in the same space;
lovers falter, or turn in video composure,
the weight of unmet expectations
heavy in the hands, the feet; bad taste in the mouth
contributes to redefinition of *other* as *obstacle*;
perfection soured, dreams of rain and unfinished business,
the sub-total of individuals before division,
a mathematics of the heart and its disease.

NETWORK

"I plan to network with everybody in sight."
— *interview subject on anti-nuke radio program*

Reticular, caught in the web
of fine blood vessels at the back of the eye,
consider vision as motion outward,
thus leave the viewer's image on the world,
take a good look each time, or vice versa;

nuclear fixation, a bad voodoo chant,
attempt to control what maybe can't be contained,
fugitive, unsatisfying, the shove toward power
frantic what-you-see-is-what-you-get is

the larger-than-life paper shredder blows the whistle,
disposing with plans, preparations, the evidence
mushroom-hammered by a white death cloud,
radioactive confetti for the final conjugal knot—
        you and whose army?—
Baron Samedi sends his regards
(evil smile on that horn-rimmed face),
whispers our familiar names, silhouette
in the light of the big bang theory at the end of the tunnel;

until the eyes have had it; how the senses work—
five;   horse;   non;   common—

(Imagine a grid placed over the world—to see in the mind—
where lines intersect: the points of greatest tension,

also where the strength is centred;
holds together as it pulls apart)

a system of conjunction, relation, the roof of a tent,
but after no holds barred, nothing remains intact;
disconsolate, the good-will ambassadors
weep into their diplomatic pouches,
even the finest escape routes become useless;

a planet with a lit candle on its head,
a *conclusive* silence, that is "caused by"
the rapid splitting of atoms, intent to disintegrate,

there's no getting around it, eventually
we will have to cross a bridge to get home.

BIRDS, LEDGES

for Tom Egan

"Nowadays his activities are mostly directed towards climbing for
its own sake, wherever it may be found, however insignificant the
rocks against the background as a whole."
> — *Mountains and Mountaineering, Guinness*

1.

Summer comes one day at a time,
a hundred birds outside, mostly sparrows
then starlings, pigeons, violet-green swallows and a pair of crows;

do the juniper berries ferment in their gizzards,
get them drunk while I barricade the garden?
Lettuce and peas attacked, spinach eaten down to the roots
(at 8:15 on Channel 3, *The Fallen Sparrow*).

He's already been dead longer than I knew him alive,
so how does this work? What's the connection?

I researched accounts of the accident in microfilm files,
the local newspaper gave it a dozen sentences,
didn't know he'd once rigged ropes from the attic window
to climb the back of his house.

"As" as in mountain, the split between urban and wilderness;
impossible to keep his pace I fell back,
followed blazes to the turquoise glacial lake
careful to step on the uphill side of rocks
down the scree slope to where he was already at home;

but, nervous in the city, examining buildings for an escape route, up.
None of the above; all of the above; infinite sky
above and below
water, the Columbia River a wet blue streak
actually colourless but reflecting blue
and the tiny moving image of a single-engine Cessna.

To know as a type of ledge, a horizontal
resting place against verticals and gravity (pulling down)

more than simply climb, he became a part of the mountain,
understood the impact of steel piton hammered
into rock fissure, bolts placed—
an arcane knowledge of names, prescribed routes, ascending paths.

A hummingbird attracted to a red wool cap
on a glacier 2500 metres above the unseen Pacific,
the same day he fell into a crevasse
(saved by the sole of his boot wedged into the ice).

"Ancient Roman bird-watchers formed a society of augurs . . .
told the future from various auspices or signs
such as the flight and appearance of certain birds."

Facts:
the airplane struck a power line above the river;
his neck snapped on impact; the other three drowned;

cars, people travelling the highway thought it was a stunt at first.

Hired to do the groundwork we raked leaves,
weeded flower beds or planted,
winter in Victoria, the rain seemed endless,

his nickname Eagle, his reputation as a crazy driver,
a green pickup loaded with shovels, rakes, pruning saws.

A lens flare illuminates the photo of him leading up the slope,
the consequence of unintentionally chosen music:
Sparrowfall 1, 2 and 3 by Brian Eno.

To let you know and subsequently say
facts repeat themselves along lines, looped vectors;
geography beneath the surface, anxious to perform,
what is a day, a decade, the lifetime of a person or a sparrow
in the single-word vocabulary of stone?

The alley choked with Morning Glory, white trumpet bell flowers;
birds bathe in dust, swallow the smallest bits of gravel;

the waitress said she had no memory for faces, then proved it.

He was talking to me when I suddenly remembered he was dead;
he asked why I was crying and I told him.
"Yes," he said, "but I'm still around,"

and he became being, the brightest verb of all.

2.

The luggage is frequently unpacked, then packed
and put away again. More than ceremony,

construction of a line composed of single points
planes into three dimensions, the addition of

the drunken apple floats in the grass beneath the tree,
during the day sparrows gather along the branches

or the body claimed by his father and taken east for burial,
a brother arrived to drive the dream car, now his, also east;

my legacy was a pair of fingerless climbing gloves
made that way to get the surest grip, "In China,

after the west wind, dogs die, chickens die, trees get sick"
Mr. Tam, in a striped pyjama shirt, works in the garden,

birds avoid people, home is where the home is,
"A falling climber gathers energy as long as he gathers speed,"

an indefinite article, attention to the configuration of rock,
or a rising cloud of wings, soprano voices singing somewhere

END OF A SEASON

"... when I arose to go
Her fingers were like the tissue
Of a Japanese paper napkin."
— from "The Encounter" by Ezra Pound

The garden is already emptied
despite its promise.
of endless giving;

the sky grows cold at night,
days are cool,
brisk as the snap of flame
in a pile of burning leaves.

Trying to sprout new seeds
would be foolish now,
when everything stretches
away from the centre of summer;

an old glove
dissolves into the earth,
and fingers, like sandpaper,
brush across my cheek
for the last time
as I close the gate behind me.

BORROWING SCENERY

"Borrowed scenery" is an aspect of Chinese and Japanese gardening, in which architecture or topography from outside a garden is incorporated into its design.

"According to the 1635 CE Chinese garden manual, *Yuanye*, there are four categories of borrowing: *yuanjie* ('distant borrowing,' e.g. mountains, lakes), *linjie* ('adjacent borrowing,' neighbouring buildings and features), *yangjie* ('upward borrowing,' clouds, stars), and *fujie* ('downward borrowing,' rocks, ponds)."

—Wikipedia

ALWAYS

something about the sky,
the quality of light specific, not released
but held against my heart which hears your name, possibly
music rising into blue,
the thin flannel of cloud,
parallel lines fan out to wind-filled afternoon
sky, imaginary, the last of summer,
expands the smell of dry leaves into the September air,
a mess of fallen plums and wasps in the back yard,
bronze fruit sweet as honey you said, maybe sweeter.

AS IF READING A TRANSCRIPT
FROM A DISTANCE

(for my father)

One afternoon, I arrive at the hospital bed,
your sleeping frown and lungs' noisy dream of oxygen
(green-blue tube draped over ears, into nostrils)

the silhouette of you beneath blanket, diminished,
no legs below the knees and whatever else remains
        shrinking fast.

But I don't want to wake you,
compliant with the obstacle to conversation
we've constructed so precisely.

No call for words to fill old blanks
in my confession of absence—

the look of no surprise
when you wake and see me waiting.

A FEW LAST WORDS

(for T.W.W.)

Gentle curve of country music on the radio,
You are my sunshine arcing across prairie sky,
remember, a big blue Plymouth,

but now, where is this place?
A long way from wheat fields
or the garage, a voice down the hall
says it's time to go, be ready
(as if you could),

> Was this departure too early? Always
> got us there sooner than anyone else
> but never put himself ahead of others.

crawling underneath the engine of some car
"Just a moment," you might say—
only this time you've disappeared,
won't be asking for a wrench or
the trouble light, instead

your oil-darkened hands are open, emptying
back into the sound of your name,
we picture you, smiling and so happy.

HEIRLOOM

All morning my son brings gifts:
an imaginary candy,
a bite of his Chinese pancake
with green onion, black bean sauce

or makes coloured footprints on the blue toy slate,
says, "Here, take it"
arms full of what seems at first to be nothing
but where he stands
still for a moment,
arches at instep rise and curve
like the entrance to his museum,
doors and windows wide open,
"A present," he says, seriously
offering his smile—
        a breeze that lifts the curtains—
and everything he holds.

A PLACE TO LIVE

(for David Zieroth)

The time arrives to find
a new apartment,
but I don't know why

heat rises, steam
forced through silvered radiators
in this old building, a friend

says there is a vacancy,
an elderly woman has left her place
forgotten her furniture, her clothes;

he and I climb carpeted stairs,
autumn pattern of red leaf and gold,
the door already unlocked,

at first the rooms feel too old—
hardwood floors, dark pine,
hazel and maple-grained suite;

I notice his new family sitting quietly
as he gestures to me: look around,
so I do,

and in the bedroom
where broad windows
frame copper clouds

resting on the sky and sea beneath,
a wave of unspecific nostalgia
catches the breath

I was about to take,
motion without waking sound, an instinct
from somewhere, waiting to usher me in.

THE SPELL

In Dublin, we relax our grip
on luggage and travel, intention
having brought us this far, at last,
through skies blue or grey, no turbulence
to speak of, and here
the sun shines for minutes at a time,
till bright clouds hurry over the green hedge,
the stone wall,

later, in the Stag's Head or the Widow Scallan's
we hoist a glass of dark Guinness,
thick and malty, sweet as pudding;
well, possibly I exaggerate,
can't recall the name of the pub:
but I remember well the thatched roof
and smokers gathered outside,
in a boil of conversation

separate from us—the foreign visitors
who create our own version of this place,
streets, sounds and smells, the names
of shops and churches,
chimney pots, painted doors
all part of the spell,
the periodic incantation of this place
new and far away and here.

HERONS

Fine hairs, interlocked
on the wing feathers,
a careful weave of white
    long-legged herons
    knee-deep in Kamo River,

the hollow bones,
bodies lean enough for flight

still, I never notice them in air,
always appearing in streams
or flooded rice fields,
quiet as the snow I imagine
    draped over Mt. Fuji.

BIG STUDY (1)

At the university, *dà xuè*, of course
the students all ride bikes
and naturally the teachers also cycle:

one for T'ai Qi every morning at six sharp,
another for caligraphy, the history of this written language
evident in the shape of change through centuries;

Miss Yao laughs like the young woman she is
teaching foreigners Mandarin,
the Beijing accent, although this is farther south,
that peculiar "ar-ar-ar" a mouthful of marbles here
but marbles from the capital, so we learn

it's illegal now to publish the Chinese numerals
according to Mr. Tan, and when a student asks
how to say "my drain is plugged," he mis-hears,
writes quick characters on the blackboard
then translates as "my dream has begun."

The Mandarin word for "university" is "dà xuè", literally: big study.

BIG STUDY (2)

White hair, face smooth as a character stroke,
teacher Li explains the art of writing,
counts his blessings, numbered
from the day after twenty years of re-education—
hard work not the problem,
but leap-frog hunched in rice paddies
or hands twisted around peasant plow
instead of *mao bi*, caligrapher's brush

opposite his name seal,
also in red:
"big pine snow"
what he calls his leisure stamp
to suggest the peace
he prays for now,
a gilt ceramic Buddha in his studio room
hidden inside a cut-out cardboard box
of imported ginseng.

BIG STUDY (3)

The language class for beginners,
for me, more complex than a music lesson
simply to learn the tones:

> flat, rising, dipping, falling

in speech
makes the difference between "to be"
and "poem"

ting bù dong—I hear but don't understand;
forgive me, I am a foreigner
my tongue twists, my ear
feels a thousand *li* from my mind,
where it takes so long to translate
every answer lost in the question following.

TEA

Dark, wet leaves climb
the cup's rim, like slugs
ascending white porcelain,
escape from scalding water
or into fiery mouths
of two blue dragons,
thin clouds of mist
rise in the cold room,
across the tongue,
carry the mystery
up inside the head

to reveal a small bronze Buddha
in meditation, in verdigris,
ingesting this moment,
how good it tastes, the steaming liquid
and its fragrant transformation.

IN TRANSIT, GLORIOUS

More battle than race, pushing through streets on bicycles,
my son in a bamboo child-seat behind me,
which is women's style, not men's, but I'm a foreigner
so add it to the list of my mistakes,
anyway I'm too busy following my sister-in-law, YuYing
along Hundred Step Alley then into other streets,
each larger than the one I turn from and busier
so I feel like a twig swept up in currents, keep checking Sean
to make sure he doesn't catch a foot in the wheel and just because
we're in this together (he's fine of course, enjoying the ride).
Then on Phoenix Street, where everyone does a slow crawl,
go and stop and go, around tiny, red TianJin taxis, etcetera,
a motorcycle almost collides with a bus, or the other way around—
who can tell?—the motorcyclist's elbow
the only thing hurt, still an argument erupts
between him and the bus driver,
passengers joining in to shake fingers
at the two-wheeler, who eventually raises his hands,
a gesture to the crowd for support, gets instead a dressmaker
out on the sidewalk to wave her yardstick at this individual,
shame, shame to impede the crowded bus,
until he surrenders and accepts blame,
guilt and innocence decided in the real people's court.

WITNESS

Mr. High-hope climbs rungs above the street
to dust painted characters meaning "good eats;
good fortune" framing his restaurant door,
behind his back, a camera.

Huò cuán, low, flat freight barge
passes under the stone bridge,
down the ancient canal,
water slow and thick
with the production of steel,
oil for revolution's bearings, its wandering
still lined with camphor trees
and white-flowered jasmine
masking bright sun or greasy haze.

So get it straight—the shot, light from the margins
puts brilliance into his black hair,
stretches a shadow from the small girl,
her pigtails braiding umbrage
to the foot of father's ladder.

DUST (CHÉN TU)

It's the dominant product
of 1.2 billion pairs of feet, or bicycle tires,
or the daily grind
of how many buses, trucks, taxis
and (these days) private cars?

The air is chalky
with smoke from iron furnaces,
and fine powder clouds blossoming
around enormous concrete factories,
one in every town, it seems;

while in narrow alleys, humble streets,
small braziers burn soft-coal tablets
to cook rice or heat water for tea.

The grit of deconstruction, too,
along the canals
where ancient homes are torn down,
clay and plaster crumbling
over splintered wood, pungent
with family histories.

Easy for an outsider
to develop nostalgia for an imagined life
glazed under ash, air
heavy with incense, a soft filter
of light and murmur, this atmospheric grain
conditional, taking shape without end,

a faded, red silk banner
or the unreadable grandmother half in,
half out of the dark entrance,
settled on that short wooden stool
quietly accumulating her share of the proceeds.

WHEN SUDDENLY THE SKY

High above the mesh of right angles—streets and lanes
walled, names painted red, maybe blue, like slogans—
the curved and tiled rooftops, *fáng zi,*
dragon-ended at the ridge or plain, shapes somehow organic
but not vegetable, instead, the wings of a large bird,
the hook of collar bone or cupped hand;

laundry hangs humid on bamboo poles and loops of pink
or white plastic clothespins, resembling bunches of lychee
and longan, suspended in market shop-fronts
above baskets of yellow pear, fragrant melon;

one balcony, a community of wooden cages, tiny ladders
for parakeets and canaries, porphyry and lime green feather
against water-stained concrete, all at once
opening their throats to sing the sudden
break in the clouds, trajectory of avian voices
clearing a path all the way to heaven.

EXIT

THE SONG COLLIDES WITH THE EXIT

The song has no title. It breathes
all the oxygen in the room, but that's all right.
We sing along anyway
if we know what's good for us.
The song has no molecules,
can't be held in our hands or passed around
for a closer look.

A tumbler of cold water
waits on a table, frosted glass on mahogany
while the song takes its own sweet,
sweet occupation of our thoughts.
In the meantime, we languish,
rest in a chair, perhaps,
near the table and the drink. This is our job
we believe, humming the melody,
this is what's expected of us.

The song changes pitch and we think:
ah, yes, modulation,
happy that we know the word,
what it means. We think
this knowledge makes us wiser
than birds, who only sing
but have no dictionaries.

But the room is much too warm,
stuffy like a sweater in August,

we begin to drift, heads slowly droop,
then snap back up, but not for long
as these actions repeat. The song
relocates to the background
like Mr. Satie's furniture.

And we wake for only a moment,
noticing for the first time
the flowering wisteria in the garden, outside,
too late to respond, as the song
crashes through the exit, loud
as a drum kit dropped down a stairwell,
takes us along, shouting ineffectually,

"No thanks. Not now. Not me."
Wishing we'd been following more closely
or at least had made up some words
to that last chorus, ourselves.

GEOLOGY OF HOME

The abstract flavour of a place:
salt air, sweet water,
qualities that feed days
and grow into years,
shed layers of fine dust, a carpet
of hemlock needles, lacy fans
from cedar branches splayed like doilies
across the bench that offers
a perspective lesson: A. the viewer's eye,
B. a pod of red and yellow kayaks
out on the inlet's blue surface,
C. the distant ridges
that either find their way to mountains
or step down to the shore,
depending.

Voices that sing or speak or laugh,
argument and agreement both
layered, too, less tangible soil
of a different growth:
boy to man,
family into what
the story allows, following
rules of narrative tempered,
softened into folds of a blanket
embroidered like needlepoint sampler:
        Harmony and Dissonance,
        Plainsong and Chorus.

HOW TO STAY ON THE TRAIL

Begin wherever you are,
but first look around,
notice the configuration of living things:
trees, ferns, flowering shrubs,
the varieties of green (too numerous
to be considered a single colour),
how sun streaks down through the cedars,
so you will recognize the place
if you should find yourself
back there at any time.

Keep your eyes focused on the middle distance,
breathe deeply but gently,
resting your tongue
against the roof of your mouth,
completing a kind of circle.

Walk at first, to introduce your feet to the ground,
then run a bit to learn what it feels like,
and as you move along through forest
(or across a meadow of loosestrife and cattail,
with that jitterbug of insect wings,
or over barnacle-crusted rocks at water's edge)
whisper a song to give yourself hope, direction,
light to see by—all these things contained in music.

Let the lower half of your thinking
drop behind occasionally to observe

where you've already passed, what condition
you've left the landscape in.
Move forward with care, pay attention
to the passage of time—you'll want to consider this
when the way grows confusing.

And when the sky becomes too dark
to see beyond the reach of your arms,
stop and build a fire.
Sit on a rock or log and contemplate the flames,
the way they remind you of voices you've heard,
of everything you've seen,
while you wait for the trail to open up again,
radiant and slightly unfamiliar
with the rising of the fog.

IN THE HOUSE BESIDE THE CREEK

Innocence

At night, the ambient crash of creek
more percussive brush-on-snare-drum now
than when it competes with daylight
fills the room with insistence that all is well,
sleep tight, dream lavishly, there is water
in the world and in my somnolent thoughts
I ride the white rush of liquid
into the arm of the sea below our house,
the moon a luminous landing strip across
to who knows what waits
over there, where mystery opens
like a grin, a wish, a sound
landscape of possibility.

Experience

So glad we don't
live next door—that house
with its bad *feng shui*
water running underneath, whisking
good fortune and tranquility out to sea
tonight especially, after all
this rain: a foam, a froth
of torrent down the creek bed
500 times its normal volume
still not enough to drown out
the young woman in pink stretch pants
outside her kitchen entrance, crying
into the telephone—all that water, that noise—
"It's my life, too," she says
just next door.

THAT MOUNTAIN

My grandfather showed up last night—
    new face and no glasses
    watching TV and, as I told him,
    looking pretty good for someone over 100.

I wonder why I don't visit him more often,
    especially when he lives so close to my home,
    and why I haven't taken my son
    to meet his only great-grandfather

and the three new cousins who answered the door,
    a happy surprise, their mother,
    my aunt—all so familiar looking
    in the quiet house, clock ticking in another room.

Grandpa asks for his favourite meal:
    pork chops and fried potatoes,
    which makes me think of the decades long
    workout his cast-iron skillet has endured.

I'm happy to oblige him now
    as I was twenty-five years ago when I last saw him,
    that visit the only time ever he travelled by plane,
    and looking out my living room window, asked,
    "Didn't that mountain use to be over there?"
    pointing miles to the east,

where he had come from to the West Coast.
    I told him I thought he was foxy,
    trying to make everyone think he'd lost his bearings,
    or misplaced them occasionally.

He just laughed—a wonderful sound—
    so familiar to me, this man I've loved all my life.
    If he comes back again, I'll cook for him whatever he likes,
    even do my best to move that misplaced mountain.

TURNED AROUND

She gets turned around,
she says, finds herself
moving away from where she wants to go,
claims that roads change direction
behind her back,

still, she follows the gravel path
down toward a cable-strung bridge,
swaying across a chasm,
green home to pounding water that moves
so fast it makes her dizzy,

she says, she can't detour
only travel straight ahead,
then steps down,
rolls her foot on an egg-shaped pebble
and falls, slowly,
like a rectangle of cloth, collapsing

tears the knee of her new beige slacks,
scrapes her hand—blood blossoms
in time-lapse tempo, tiny
beaded flowers on white skin;

not easy, she says, not fair
to have no sense of direction,
when the world is a web of paths
passing through light and dark,

a series of melting landmarks
that double back on themselves,
confusion a game
she has no choice but to play.

THE DISTANCE FROM THE CHAIR
TO THE FLOOR

I am falling and I cannot rise
in this pressure inversion, no condor
or turkey vulture will soar,
so clearly I will continue in descent;

the precious moments left are perhaps countable,
but barely a thought can be crowded
into this little package of time, and see,
see how the broadloom looms,
the hard landing beckons.

This is all and all that is left
is to hit, hard, collapse onto the floor,
bewildering destination
and the recognition that
the instant before the fall
can never be regained.

2 WEST: PALLIATIVE CARE

Pale blue walls and paintings
of boats moored somewhere in sun
below a whitewashed village, draining itself into the sea—
but outside your window, snow piles up laboriously,
weather working overtime, lighting
with a grey wash, the room, the bed,
a mother diffused,

your wig gone, stuffed into a plastic bag
with glasses, magazines I brought,
the clothes you wore when you arrived here,
not expected, only a week ago,
no time, it seems, barely enough to say goodbye,
your almost final words to me yesterday:
"I'm not much company, am I?"

Now, you chase your own breath inside an oxygen mask,
cough, and your eyes fly open, you look
startled to be here but who knows
what you really see?
I take your hand, skin like dried egg white,
touch your cheek, hot with the effort of waiting,

out in the ward, a woman shouts
look at me—look at me,
and a phone rings, unanswered

so, as with every death, the end of a dialogue,
this one, though,
the longest conversation of my life
incomplete, left hanging.

THE FINE POINT

Insistent,
argument invades
like a sliver of glass,
or how my mother told me a needle
could travel, that is
if you stepped on one,
embedded it in the flesh
beneath your heel,
the metal would begin to move upward
like a silver-scaled fish
swimming against gravity
through the muscle at the back of the leg
and up the length of thigh
into torso, nosing its way
toward a vital organ—
liver, spleen or heart, perhaps—
intent on finding a resting place
a spawning ground for the discomfort
of its host, who remains
unaware of this menace
remembering only the slender stab
felt once, back when foot
inherited the fine point,
the beginning of an end
established itself in the blood
and meat of distraction.

PEACH

At its centre, this spherical flame
concentrates itself,
combustion pressing inward,
so keenly it forms an almost-cosmic implosion,
black hole, the bitter arsenic of rage
pounded into a wrinkled stone.

Lava flows in veins
beneath the cortextual topography,
the frowning surface an illusion
of calm, of indecision,

hides the poorly-made choice—
the wrong thing done at the wrong time—
a shouted challenge, the scrape
of painted metal against metal
a fracture in the flow of traffic;
think hard before action
is a thought that comes too late
to the peach;

a fine sweetness suggesting summer,
orchard cool green against the heat,
each branch weighed down
with a knot of fire and
a callous heart.

VIRTUE DEFICIT

Muddied
by lack of self-discipline I
can't finish a line
or make it to the end of the stanza
        (down the pier, into deeper water)
without digression,

and though Miles Davis said,
"never complete a phrase,"
I imagine this advice
is less than pocket change for a writer
        (nickel, dime or lowly penny)

and so attempt again
        (like some diet addict)
a trajectory through the overlapping folds
of previous effort
to find an entrance to virtue,
even a small one:
flake of responsibility,
speck of perseverance,
courage enough

to complete the sentence
        (do the time) as if
this matters, and matters most
the magnificent gift of knowing for a moment
a thing done properly,
done well.

WIND

When that wind climbed inside the legs of my pants,
billowing cuffs, rattling change
in my pockets, keys, a lucky stone
smooth as a seal's eye with the rubbing of my fingers,
but yes, that breeze

the one that shook the yellow frilling flowers
from the maples into roof gutters and across the drive,
spun whitecaps up from the cove's floor
to water's surface,
chased the neighbours inside from their deck,
where they'd been about to eat lunch,

that was the storm that woke something,
blew open a sheaf of curtain closed too long,
rooms dim and stale as old bread—
a shaggy bristling discomfort.

But now the air is calm; what was passing has passed,
left me standing in rain-cooled afternoon,
thick clouds rolling eastward while I try to catch blessings
and balance them long enough to count.

BEAR PROOF

Not the seedy, pie-plate
splat of shit on the lawn
or the branch torn ragged
from the yellow plum tree
and left, mangled, at the top
of the driveway;

nor the plastic trash can,
lid punctured by mighty teeth
designed to tear flesh from bone,
then splinter that bone for its marrow heat,
never mind the remnants of garbage
rejected as unfit for even a bear to eat,
swatted, strewn among flowering shrubs,
rhododendron now draped with plastic shopping bag,
coffee filters, something slimey, undistinguishable,
no, not this time,

but this:
the visitor himself, mid-day lumbering calm
up the street toward the trees
where he will solve the problems
a bear in the woods must face
in order to prove himself at home,
the end of a busy day.

HUMMINGBIRD

This yard is an avian gingerbread house
in a sloping West Coast forest
with terraced banks of garden—
yellow, violet and red, mostly
red that calls the hummingbirds
busy sewing up the morning light,
attaching themselves to temptation,
bee balm and fuchsia semaphore
lures them here

where cats' claws and mindless
leap twist grab from air
becomes the unjust reward.

My complicity unavoidable, flies up too,
locks grip with guilt, proceeds to anger,
ridiculous, I know, to be enraged
simply by cats being cats,
frustrating my attempts to protect birds
with useless belled collars,
limited yard time, supervised like convicts

and then I hear their calls at the door
where I find them staring, almost surprised,
at a now-still vibration of green
which, in my hand is weightless and warm,
its beak a tiny hairpin
partly open, wanting to speak, to sing out
against this undeserved end,
how unfair, how much my fault.

BIRDBRAIN

Little birdbrain
on a happy swoopdown
from cedar branch, you sing
along the way until
bang, you hit
full speed into window
glass, I guess, reflecting garden,
an inviting space to glide through
but that geography of morning
air somehow solid
so there you drop,
leave a feathered thumbprint
on the patio door
to mark your surprise
and my dismay.

LOOSE

On this sunlit, unreliable day
I bolt like a kid skipping school,
collaborate with the subtraction that is autumn

leave the building and the car behind,
wander out to find a new neighbourhood,
down sidewalks, across sculpted lawns

examine shrubbery shaped into cartoon fetishes
as a woman watches from a window:
the sight of this stranger in her yard;

and a courier in a van
waits impatiently for me to cross the street
while I think simple thoughts that lead to

green qualities of light through trees and air
(the exhalation of their breath) a tide
that holds the distant inlet up against breakwater;

a fishing boat enters the gleaming basin
like a bold stranger,
smoothes its way across the surface,

someone's pantleg gathers like a flag in the breeze
then unfurls in strides along the walkway,
down steps and into the park.

My concern for today and tomorrow:
the boy who will be home, waiting
for my return: the father

like a lost dog, running
through streets without purpose
except to run, to run—

no excuse but the scent
of some new thing just ahead
to keep me going.

TOTAL RECALL

All the actions, large as airship balloons
that keep growing while losing colour

or slight movement that perhaps
the eye can't follow

the steps up toward the front
of a vaguely red house

or grey, no building matters
in this story,

because when I look back
behind me to consider the pattern

of grass bent, arranged neatly
into the shape of a path taken

I see nothing, an open
empty expanse of lawn, and

everything I did
isn't there.

TRACEY CALLS

I just got another call from TRACEY who called because she was asked by SEARS to call people out of the blue (which happens to be the colour of the shirt I'm wearing today), and find out what sorts of thoughts they might have about SEARS stores. She sounded like a nice person, so I wasn't rude to her and I didn't threaten to call the police to get her to stop harassing me. Instead, I told her I'd think about SEARS as much as possible in the next few days and I'd get back to her.

Yes, I was lying, but I don't think I'll burn in HELL for a little white lie.

I mentioned it was "another call" because someone called me on Friday and I'm pretty sure that was TRACEY, too. But I told her then I was much too busy with IMPORTANT MATTERS to spend any time discussing a department store with her. Another lie (about the important matters). I guess it's true what they say: tell a lie and they start piling up all over the place.

I feel sorry for TRACEY and all her telephone soliciting brethren and sistren. It's not her fault that SEARS wants to know my thoughts about their stores, and will pay her GOOD MONEY to find out.

I think that what she does is a little bit like FISHING, only a darker, weirder, more intrusive kind of fishing than I've ever done.

HOODAH NERUDA

I wake in petulance, a dream of licking the sky
while pale fish find new avenues to wander,
the whole of my pitiful self displayed
on a table, with a chair nearby, shames me

as fragments of a life—my life—
flip past in blurry cinema presentation,
black-framed screen means brilliant zeros
unless you understand the language of disjunction:

here a hand moves under cloth, reveals the mystery
somebody coughs and breaks the spell
of disbelief suspended,
all that's gone undetected till now

does any poor soul see the performance
behind the white platform, a stage raised
into a vertical sequence of notes and shivers,
the unmistakable smell of something burning,

possibly the starving dogs are waiting to join
bears and coyotes who dine on neighbourhood cats,
mothers in place behind glass and glaze
over the scene in their back yards

my skimpy wishes never get dressed,
never leave the house to enter the world;
but the world comes to me instead.
This time on earth, this passionate hoodah.

BEARS

Always in this darkened landscape
where the bush grows to road's edge,
they are certain to appear:
grizzlies with ferocious, humped shoulders
or blacks and their cinnamon coloured cousins,
pursue me, follow, and
in the wake of my dreamy walking,
just as I know they will,
come out from between the alders, parting branches
resolute and quiet behind me on the path,
maintaining bear presence in peripheral light

so I speed up, head for the house quickly, carefully,
without running because that would only make them run, too,
my feet raising small puffs of dust, I imagine
but don't turn back to look, or consider
just what house this is, or whose, or how
I know it's here,
still they trail me to the flimsy screen door.

I lock it anyway, which seems ridiculous but
sometimes keeps them out, circling the house
peering in windows with squinty, myopic eyes,
though often they find an opening and I know
they're inside, maybe the kitchen, clearing out the fridge
or shredding the living room furniture with curved yellow claws

I feel their movement, smell the rank aroma of old grease
or find a tuft of fur on a door jamb,
I want to get away but where is there to go?
back outside? further inside? into a closet or down to the basement?
this house, wherever it is, I suddenly realize
is never enough to keep me separate from their intent,
those bears, unsettled night, the looming day that waits.

ACKNOWLEDGEMENTS

I am very grateful to the editors of the following publications who have published many of the poems in this collection (some in slightly different form):

Event, Descant, The Fiddlehead, Grain, The Malahat Review, The New Quarterly, Poetry Strand, Pottersfield Portfolio, The Raddle Moon, West Coast Line, Writing.

Thanks also to the editors and publishers at Arsenal Pulp Press (*East of Main: An Anthology of Poems from East Vancouver*); and Tsunami Editions (*Visualized Chemistry*), where some of the poems also appeared.

Many thanks to my friends and colleagues at Douglas College and at the University of British Columbia for their comments and suggestions.

And finally, I would like to acknowledge the tremendous support and generosity of Tom Wayman and David Zieroth.